WRITE THE NEIGHBOURHOOD

WRITE THE
NEIGHBOURHOOD

*Essays from our global
community*

EDITED BY ANNABEL TOWNSEND

The Penny University Press

First Printing, 2024 by Pete's Press

Dedicated to the 'neighbourhoods' where our writers have found their homes;
and to the loved ones they find in them.

Contents

REGINA, SASKATCHEWAN

KWAZULU-NATAL, SOUTH AFRICA

KENNEDY, SASKATCHEWAN

SHROPSHIRE, UK

REGINA, SASKATCHEWAN

THE END

I

⚜

Introduction: Thirteen

BY ANNABEL TOWNSEND

A couple of years ago in the autumn of 2021, I hid in my office at the back of the bookshop to record an interview for a friend's new chat show. The host, David, is like me: someone who collects people. Not in the creepy serial killer sense, I promise — just in the sense that he enjoys other people's stories. His chat show was filled with interviews with local folk who he finds interesting. And apparently I am interesting.

My bookstore, situated on 13th Avenue in Regina, is housed in an older - but not heritage - building roughly in the centre of the neighbourhood. Although as spacious as I can afford, we have enough books and trinkets crammed in there that it feels cosy and somehow old-fashioned. The office was a cramped mess of boxes of overstock, and many paper bags labeled with "spare display stuff" or "more elastic bands". A crate of Christmas decorations sat forlornly in the corner. The shelf, precariously stacked high with books that haven't sold, (and consequently, bowing under the weight of the author's disappointment, too) looked ready to fall at any moment. The lighting was too dim for the video, which was possibly a relief given my slovenly backdrop.

I matched my surroundings: disheveled, disorganised and on the verge of collapse. My staff and colleagues were well aware - not only of the bombsite aesthetic in the office, but also of my acute stress levels. It wasn't long before they staged an intervention. My office has now been forcibly tamed and tidied. I did "help" move things- the mess of boxes still exists, but it now exists in my attic at home, and for my eyes only. Everything in the office is now specifically placed, conscientiously and regimentally. But it is still dim in there, and the eclectic mix of random things that no one ever realises that a bookstore needs, such as plastic crows, empty plant pots, a hammer and a broken claw machine contain eggs filled with snippets of poetry, still crowd every surface.

Now though, the office contents can be perceived as *creative clutter*, and it makes suitable lodgings for eccentric writers. Perhaps unsurprisingly, I am feeling a lot less stressed.

But back to the chat show. David had been stalking me prior to the interview. He found my author website, read some of my ramblings, and noticed the part where I claim to be influenced by the discipline of *psychogeography*. His first question to me was,

"What on earth is Psychogeography?"

psy·cho·ge·og·ra·phy
/ˌsīkōjēˈägrəfē/
noun
the study of the influence of physical and geographical environment on the mind or on behavior.

***

Psychogeography is not usually confined to one single office, however. For many years, I have been interested in the way your surroundings - the local community, the neighbourhood, the weather - all affect your mood and behaviour. I have lived in Regina, Saskatchewan for twelve years now, but as an immigrant from the UK, at times I still feel like an alien in the parts. During the chat show interview, David expressed his dismay at why anyone would voluntarily *choose* Regina. Another friend rolls her eyes whenever I say anything enthusiastic about winter, as 'the locals' dread it and tend to hibernate. I know this city is a long way from perfect, but I do unashamedly love it.

Regina is not large, in fact, by European standards it would barely be considered a *city* at all, but by subconscious design, I have made my world even smaller. The centre of my universe is now a singular neighbourhood in Regina: the area immediately surrounding the west end of 13th Avenue known as Cathedral. "Thirteen" holds special - albeit contrived - significance to me as well: my first Canadian job was at 13th Avenue Coffee House. We moved into our first proper home here in 2013. Our eldest child's birthday is on the 13th. My husband and I had been together for 13 years when we emigrated. If there are such things as serendipitous signs, this was definitely one of them.

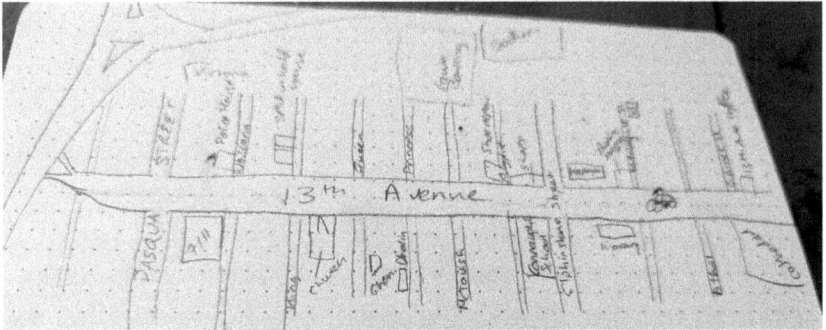

13th Avenue map - not even remotely to scale.

A brief stroll, - or *derive* ('drift') as psychogeographers call it - to the east on 13th takes you through one of the city's oldest neighbourhoods. Almost everything here, including the eponymous Cathedral, was rebuilt after a tornado flattened it in 1912, making the majority of buildings and homes at least a century old. Again, coming from the UK, it took me a while to get used to the concept of one-hundred year-old buildings being classed as 'Heritage'. Canada is such a young nation-state!

The residential streets are now punctuated with more modern infill housing and deliberately gentrified facilities. As such, the area is not so much a product of streamlined, holistic urban design, but a mash-up of the individual whims, dated architectural fashions and contrasting incomes of its home-building residents, neatened up by the arterial roads that nudge it into a reluctant grid. But despite the obvious city-owned and designed infrastructure, what makes the area unique are the little pockets of fallible human influence on this topologically-challenged prairie city.

With rather lapse planning laws to contend with, I enjoy seeing how colourful the houses are. Garnet Street, that runs at ninety degrees to 13th has two of my favourite houses on it: one is a three-storey old house painted brightly, almost violently, purple, and opposite it, further up the road is a smaller, unassuming bungalow with Doctor Who's TARDIS in the front yard. 13th Avenue itself boasts a deep orange hair salon, a purple baby supplies place, and a lime green, baby blue and pink painted ice cream parlour. The vegetarian restaurant has a mural of cows on the side wall, all with blank Stop signs for faces. Other murals dot the sides of businesses and buildings on both sides of the street, and steel sculptures in primary colours pop out at pedestrians on the sidewalk. It is all delightfully, eccentrically, cheerful.

On the blocks closer to Albert Street, the main thoroughfare that provides an unspoken border to the neighbourhood, things begin to get a little weirder. On my most recent walk, I noticed an entire dining set - Formica table and matching chairs - set up next to a dumpster in the alley. On Retallack St., someone keeps a 12 foot high plastic skeleton in their front yard, year round. Last year, a dead squirrel, eyes sunken, its body rigid and frozen, lay in the alley for months after it apparently electrocuted itself chewing on the power lines. On the power line pole itself, in between the Lost Cat posters and the multitude of ancient staples, are a far stranger pair of stickers. "#Skies" one says, followed by "This is our Jihad." The other is even more unhinged and lacks any decipherable context: "Strange white powder that never melts." I could make a guess at what sort of white powder may have inspired these stickers, but I think in this case, the sticker refers to snow. Underneath there is a hyperlink to a website titled 'GeoEngineeringWatch'.

Parts of the sidewalk on the southern edge of 13th Avenue are almost impassable, caked in solid ice after the regular cycles of melt-and-freeze, melt-and-freeze that make up what passes for a Saskatchewan spring. I do the 'penguin walk', knees bent, centre of gravity as low to the ground as I can muster, small, sliding steps. As I do so, I wonder how I ever managed to normalize this behaviour, and yet the muscle memory is there, installed in my mind, even as a foreigner in these parts. For the past few years, I have begun photographing the strange things that emerge from the ice each Spring: a miniature bottle of hand sanitizer, a felt heart, a toy Minion figure, what I think is a neon pink stitch marker from a crochet set, and most concerningly, a wooden sign with HELP ME scratched in it. (On closer inspection, this appeared to be a Halloween decoration, which may give you some idea of how long things remain frozen in this part of the world.)

So, how does this environment affect its inhabitants? The Cathedral neighbourhood does have a reputation for being the artsy, hippy area, and the stereotypes are often quite fair. Does the neighbourhood look this way because we all creative, colourful, a bit weird and prone to conspiracy theories? Possibly. Or are we slippery, frigid and unwelcoming for a long part of the year? As much as we shape our environment, it also shapes us.

In this series of essays, readers are invited on a journey through diverse landscapes, both physical and cultural. From the often dangerous streets of inner city Toronto to the remote parts of Northern Saskatchewan, and from the challenges of load shedding in South Africa to the unexpected charm of urban goat farming in the UK, this collection of essays illuminates the interconnectedness of communities worldwide. Through the lens of personal experience, these writers explore themes of resilience, community, creativity and the ever-evolving nature of our surroundings. "Write the Neighbourhood" is not just a collection of stories, but a testament to the power of storytelling to bridge gaps and foster understanding across borders.

Toronto, Ontario

I

Reflections from the Urban Jungle

BY LEIGHTON PEART

Photograph retrieved via christophermartinphotography.com

I was born and raised in Toronto. Growing up, my neighbour-hood was plagued by gun violence, daylight robberies, and gang activity. Being a black man represented a specific form of precari-ousness. I was often carded, as I fit the description of what the police called their "suspects." When I think of such memories, I think of the multitude of friends and acquaintances who succumbed to violence. I was adept at navigating such tumultuous situations that I never became a direct victim of them—I always existed on the periphery. When I run into old friends, it often seems like someone I once knew has passed away. I recently learned one of my friends had been gunned down in broad daylight as he exited a mosque with his family. Another friend of mine was summarily executed by a single bullet to the head as he walked his daughter through their neighbourhood one early morning. Death is not foreign to me, nor does it ever come as a surprise.

It is a peculiar feeling to know that many of your friends have perished or are in jail. It is an even more peculiar feeling to recog-nize that it could have been you in that cell or grave. I am by no means glamorizing the life of gang violence and murder. In fact, I am admonishing it. Many of my friends had similar upbringings to mine. Single parent households, truancy and delinquent in school efforts, and having little to no support system. One should not doubt a young male's desire to belong to something greater than themselves. It is a cruel truth that certain preconditions invariably led to my friends joining gangs. I can only theorize why this was the case, but I assume it is in large part due to feeling powerless against ever-growing, ever-oppressive forces. The internal struggle of want-ing to fit in, of wanting to be desired, to be cool — versus the ex-ternal struggle of assimilation, the constant pressure placed on one to be normative. Again, it is puzzling because I should have been a statistic in this regard. I've seen friends stabbed, and gunbutted by

AK47s — I've had machetes pulled on me, and somehow, I managed to walk out of these situations physically unscathed. I know people serving life sentences for murder. I know people serving lengthy prison sentences for trafficking narcotics. Again, this is not a point of pride for me. I look at it in a sobering, matter-of-fact way while acknowledging that each of us can find ourselves on our own path. Whether that path is morally right or not is not up to me to decide.

I have shed countless tears for the fallen. I spend many hours thinking of innocent times playing basketball at the local rec center or playing large games of manhunt (tag) around the local internet café. I think of sunny days turning into cold, dark nights. I think of broken lives that will never regain their original shape. I think of one decision bringing about titanic negativity. I remember myself, wanting to fit in so badly, willing to do anything to be accepted by my peers. I never sold drugs, held or used a weapon, nor did anything of the like, but so many of my friends opted for that route. Whether they knew "better" or not, I cannot safely say. Maybe it was all they knew—never once afforded a glimpse into an alternative way of being, thinking, and existing. Of course, this is all speculative. None of my murmurings will bring back my fallen brethren. These are choices they made nonetheless, and the consequences have been significant.

There are lasting psychological effects from the ordeals I have been through. I have had partners comment about how "on edge" I am, or how I seem to always be on "high alert" when we are together in public. I remember a specific instance when I was walking downtown with my partner at the time. I had eyed a black Honda with tinted windows about 200 feet away. When it drove past us in the adjacent lane, it performed a very quick U-turn, tires screeching loudly. Instinctively, I recoiled and began running for cover. Presumably, the car had missed its turn and was trying to get back on course. My partner laughed and ridiculed me — reminding me that "those things do not happen in Toronto." It was at that moment that I realized I may have a mild form of PTSD. I also realized that my partner, who was privileged enough to hail from a sheltered upbringing outside of Toronto, was completely oblivious to the things that happen to *people like me.*

In reflecting on my experiences, I have noticed an overarching theme. I have always been an observer. I watch, take mental notes, and adjust my behavior accordingly. I am smart enough to not be dumb, but dumb enough not to be smart. Those who have been raised on the streets understand where I am coming from. It is a carefully choreographed dance on the line between pain and pleasure — between life and death. This skill of navigation was never something I wanted, yet it has been instrumental to my survival. I have spent countless hours in therapy trying to discern whether I am "living" or "surviving." I have tried, in vain, to make sense of things that are senseless. I have often asked myself, "Why not me?" I spend many of my days contemplating questions that have no answer.

As I prepare to celebrate my 29th birthday, I reflect on my tumultuous upbringing and hold a moment of silence for myself and my fallen friends.

Tinamaste,
Costa Rica

2

❦

Home Within the Heart, in the Costa Rican Jungle

BY CARA AMY GOLDTHORPE

The day is closing, as I walk back along the creek that winds like a slithering snake down the centre of my property. As the light is departing, a gentle gloom filters through the jungle, that just an hour before was glowing every shade of emerald in bejewelled splendour. Yet, despite the incoming darkness, the air is alive. The song of insects is erupting to greet the sunset – and signalling to me that I should pick up the pace. Not to rush, but more out of respect for the wild forces I know call this place home. I am a guest on these lands, though I hold their legal title: a concept very strange to me, despite being a former lawyer.

I take the left turn to the overgrown trail leading home and haul myself up out of the creek bed. Barefoot, my toes grip the loamy earth, rooting down into her, helping me climb the steep incline. It focuses the mind – especially given the scorpions, snakes and spiders that can lurk on the jungle floor, I advise any visitors here "not to follow" my lead. That's my disclaimer: you do what you like, of course. But I don't embody any modern view of safety. This *is* safety to me.

At one with the forest, I find solace after the stresses of the day that have once again nearly brought me to the brink of physical and emotional breakdown. I know it's just a test – how bad do I really want this life? I've come to view ease and flow as an illusion. Success doesn't come without hard work and discipline: although you can make it a spiritual discipline to make that hard work feel easy.

Despite my fatigue, here I am walking barefoot upon the earth. I feel peace within my heart, savouring life's raw simplicity. And to me, that is what truly matters.

* * *

Let's rewind a little bit – let me give you the quick rundown of who I am and where I hope I'm going, where I am and what led me here.

It is nearly four years since I began to call Costa Rica home. Before arriving here, I could never have imagined that this is where

I would've ended up. Yet now, it is impossible to imagine an alternative.

In early 2020, I was cleaning out my messy barrister's office in preparation for a long holiday. For those not familiar with the British legal system, a barrister (not "barista", although we do often survive on a lot of caffeine) is a litigator. My bread-and-butter work ranged from inheritance disputes between high-net-worth individuals, to High Court freezing injunctions, to bankruptcies, insolvencies, and eviction proceedings.

After a year teetering on the edge of burnout, I had booked a month off. This coincidentally turned out to be just before the pandemic brought the world to a standstill, leading to my lockdown in jungle paradise. Although sounding idyllic, at the beginning of that uncertain time, I was honestly in quite the panic. Being stuck in Central America was completely unplanned. I had no means to work out here, and I was racking up costs – rentals for my London flat and office, as well as other expenses associated with my legal business.

Fast forward six months, and it became clear to me that Costa Rica was home. There was something so special that kept me here even when border restrictions lifted. I did return to Europe, and I even attempted to work in law again at one point, but the strong draw of the hot, humid wilderness pulled my soul back.

Its raw beauty made me face myself. It brought shadows into the light, it shattered my ego, it made me feel my fragile humanness, whilst simultaneously connecting my spirit with the stars. I found myself infused with a kind of insanity, as a voice from 'somewhere else' begged me to invest everything I had into a piece of the earth, regardless of the consequences. Even if it meant living in a tent with nothing else to my name. The richness of the jungle made me feel wealthy in ways money never could. It made me realize how ill I had felt in the confines of the city, trapped in a constant race of work. And it showed me a new way, a humble yet majestic way.

Two years and three failed property deals later, during which time I met the man who would become my husband and received the tremendous financial support of my parents and family, I found my spot here on planet earth. We finally completed a real estate purchase. Another eighteen months later and we are in the final stages of finishing our physical home.

At first, the vision was quite different. Our original budget was much smaller than what the build ballooned into. I wanted to start small, to build a "tiny home" so that we could gain experience with construction in Costa Rica and test the waters with our team of builders, without the pressure of a higher-budget house project. Really, I just wanted to move back onto our land as soon as possible. After purchasing it, we had lived there in an old run-down bodega for three months. We had no electricity, making fires at sundown and charging our phones from a car battery. When that got too much (and especially during rainy season), we ended up jumping from house to house in the neighbourhood, offering our services as dog-sitters, payment in-kind. We stayed in some lovely places but none of them felt like home.

I've learnt that everywhere has its imperfections – so you may as well be somewhere where the imperfections feel perfect, or at least worth putting up with. It's a kind of relationship of sorts, and I've learnt to navigate being in relationship with an acreage. Running away from this land hoping the grass would be greener somewhere else was just me running away from myself. Procrastinating and putting off facing the difficulties or doing the hard work to water my own plants, would not help manifest something real here.

* * *

We broke ground in December 2023. The very next day, I brought the work to a halt, nervous about the foundations. We experience regular earthquakes here and just the previous year, there had been a landslide on one corner of the property. Something in me wanted to start afresh, knowing that I wouldn't be able to sleep at night if we continued to build in the original spot.

After a week of delays, during which I scrambled around getting advice and second or third opinions from engineers, we re-started – only to be bombarded by unseasonal rains. They were worse than we'd had in the wet season, and it poured down just as all the timber for the project was being delivered.

I was already on the cusp of meltdown. Everyone had cautioned me against building with wood in the tropics, because of how prone it is to assault – from the elements, mold, rot, and termites. Here I was, following my heart and its yearning to build with natural materials, and already I was being put to the test. The house wasn't even built yet, and my untreated, un-oiled, unsealed wood was being besieged by water.

I remember that first night after the delivery, huddling up in the old bodega, my clothes and hair already wet from the leaking roof, feeling the earth tremble and moan (for the bodega has no solid foundations and you feel every subtle move of the tectonic plates). I remember smelling the new timber. It was covered in a tarp, but still outside. Clearly water was leaking in and pooling around the stack. I have never smelled wood like that, as though it was on fire from the water. It smelled like burning oils, potent, powerful, teasing my patience.

The following morning, we did our best to shift some of the giant timber beams into the slightly better shelter of the bodega. I didn't care about sacrificing my living space – I felt the timber as though it was my baby. It needed to be dry, it needed to be protected, so that in future it could one day protect me. I remember the sinking feeling in my heart as I noticed the warping on some of the planks that had been badly submerged in water, where the tarp had collapsed inward under the weight of the downpour and caused the rain to pool and seep in around the edges.

Soon enough, I realized there was nothing I could do. Dwelling on it would not help me solve my problems, build my house, or figure out how to clean and treat my teak wood in a country where finding the sorts of ecological products I was looking for was not easy. I began turning my attention to the future, researching how I could protect the wood, and figure out how to prove wrong all those people who were so skeptical of my choice of materials.

* * *

Dawn dances through the triangular windows of our loft bedroom. I had just been watching the horizon become a dusty pink and mauve. Rested, yet still feeling tired in my body, clinging on for the slumber of night.

I often wake feeling weighed down by responsibilities and physical exhaustion from lots of manual labour. But once I get that initial motivation to get out of bed, the energy of the day floods into me. Typically, I'll take some time to potter about the beginnings of our medicinal plant garden. Watching and studying: which buds are about to burst into bloom? And which leaves have been targeted by the ferocious scavenging of my pup?

I'm jumping around a little in the chronology of this story, and perhaps that's reflective of the way time seems to move differently here. Faster and slower at once, the days and weeks blur together although life is far from monotonous. Still, a daily routine strings the threads of the tapestry together. During dry season, the herbs and seedlings need their water. The deck which we will one day use for Kung Fu classes, yoga, meditation, and other community events, needs constant maintenance and cleaning (whilst the wood is still not fully sealed). We also scout our home for any new developments to be aware of. I am wary, ever since spotting the start of a termite invasion about a month ago. Thankfully that one was dealt with by an organic fumigator, who arrived with a gift of a giant bottle of the best homemade hot sauce I've had in a while, and who skillfully tackled those pesky wood-munchers that were treating my new house as an all-you-can-eat buffet.

The blur of time also has to do with the pup we rescued at birth and took in as our own. We found him and his brother on the property during one of those violent storms, umbilical cords still attached. We called in the New Year of 2024 with four walls of our home up (but no roof), grieving the loss of one pup, and our survivor requiring round the clock care. At that age, bottle feeding was necessary every two hours of day and night, not to mention how vulnerable he was growing up on a construction site exposed to jungle dangers.

In some ways that is when things started to fall apart, although they are now coming back together again, sweetly. I was crumbling, struggling to manage a build that was rapidly going up and up in cost, whilst totally sleep deprived. But I've seen that often things must totally break apart, so the new may bloom. Challenges are here to test the foundations upon which we build our lives, so that we can grow from ever-stronger roots.

I am still navigating the transition from all the struggles of build-ing, to enjoying my new home. Some days it is hard not to notice all the little things that went wrong; things that would be invisible to an external observer. Yet I designed this build, I hold the vision in my head. Since I'm a perfectionist, I've had to learn to continuously let go. There's a limit to what I can do, and to be honest, now I'm more focused on speed than attention to detail as we scramble to get all the wood oiled before the oncoming wet season.

It's a different kind of rush. It's not like the rat race of my former career, but rather the rush of natural cycles. As soon as the snows melt after a freezing cold Saskatchewan winter, where my husband grew up, seedlings must sprout and race to grow as strong and tall as they can be before the onslaught of the next winter, with temperatures reaching down to fifty below zero. Similarly, if I want my home to withstand the Central American wet season, I need to get the wood treated. I managed to import gallons of Tung oil – a natural, non-toxic product, used in ancient China for waterproofing ships. Unlike a varnish, which will cure and dry in a matter of hours, Tung oil takes weeks to cure and requires multiple re-applications.

* * *

It feels good to finally perch on my balcony and write – to have the softness, the spaciousness, the quiet sanctuary. It is April, and my team of workers have been gone for over a month now. The pace of our progress appears to be slowing in many ways, whilst I simultaneously gain more and more steadiness within myself. Clarity over where I am, and what I'm doing.

I realize I sent the team home prematurely. I could have pointed out more things that needed "finishing", which they could have done faster than us. But it wouldn't have been the same. It was getting to the point that, in terms of aesthetics, things were getting worse not better. I'd had enough of fighting for my voice to be heard by certain members of the team. Although my main builder was very respectful towards me, the same was not true of everyone. Project-managing a build as a woman in a 'machismo' Latin American country has brought with it many challenges, to say the least.

I am also beginning to realize how things may not be finished – for weeks, months, even years. The choice is either to pause and savour the ride or be swept up in the violent currents of continuous motion. Yes, there is a natural race, and certain things must be done ahead of the seasonal shifts. But there's a delicate balance to be struck. Whilst inaction will lead to decay, to overdo it and simply become one with the frenzy, is to lose sight of the purpose and vision of life.

Home begins and ends within the sanctuary we create. With the love, bliss and calm of the light we cultivate in our own hearts. Night and day, the summer and winter, all held tenderly together in a delicate dance beyond the mortality of time. That brings me to the grander vision of this place – it is not just our house we are building, but a community and education centre for others to come and experience the magic of the jungle we have fallen in love with. To learn in a hands-on and immersive way about natural medicine, permaculture, and spiritual practices.

To share what we want to share with others, and create this community centre, we need to make sure we embody our teachings, and that our home is a pillar of peace: each part of it developed with care and love.

* * *

There are many more stories to tell, and an unfinished house to complete, but things are nevertheless arriving at a sense of completion. The month of May is beginning, and I close off this chapter with a stunning view of a volcano, across Lake Atitlan in Guatemala.

My husband and I haven't really had much time just to ourselves all year – in between our puppy, co-living on our building site with a friend who came to work-exchange with us, and the presence of our construction team. We managed to pry ourselves away for a week – to rest and celebrate my birthday. It's strange being here in Guatemala: a place which seems to be a fusion of so many places that are home, so many places dear to my heart. My parents live with a similar view on a lake in lands far away. The climate on Lake Atitlan is a mix of hot days reminiscent of our Costa Rica home but lacking the humidity, and cool nights where we rug up beneath a pile of blankets. There are pine forests nearby, and grasses bordering the water's edge that remind of the Canadian prairies.

And so here I am reflecting on all the places that I call home, all whilst missing the place I have chosen to build my house. For that is where my heart led, and that is where I am to be for now, and my path is to lose myself in total presence tending that garden, knowing every flower and every root, and deepening my understanding of the medicines of the jungle.

We often say things like – "home is not a place but a person", or "home is within the heart", and I tend to agree – but there's more nuance to it. There are certain places which nurture us more, which we connect with more, and it's different for everyone. It's just like some flowers won't do well in a searing tropical sun, but others need that intense sun for their very survival.

We all belong to a particular ecosystem, and once we find where it is, the real work begins – to grow our roots, nourish community connections, and weave ourselves into the web. That is when I think we will find true peace: co-existing harmoniously with our people and the world around us.

Mpumalanga, South Africa

3

Happily, Unfinished

BY ERIN DERFOLDY

"It is the small things, everyday folk that keeps the darkness at bay. Simple acts of love and kindness."

-GANDALF FROM THE LORD OF THE RINGS

When I wake up, it's in an unfinished house. The floor is half done, only one set of taps work, we have hot water in the shower but not the kitchen sink and there's holes on one side of our huge A-frame farmhouse. The farmhouse is nestled on a 10 hectare property in the beautiful green lowveld Mpumalanga area, two-thirds of which is covered in macadamia trees with an apiary of over 20 bee hives and my father's carpentry workshop. It's been unfinished for

20 years, a legacy of sorts. I find myself not looking at that as a bad thing; I look at it as a testimony to the human spirit.

My dad had a dream to own his own land, build his own house and start his own farm. When I was born in 1986, we were staying in the back of a Kombi (a small van) with no back seats. A mattress had been put on the floor instead. My dad was paying off a piece of land and building his dream house out of wood. I don't have any memories of this house besides a scar on my lip where I fell down the stairs in my walker. The owner of the property that my dad was trying to buy, ended up selling the land to someone else without telling my father. He was forced to move and his dream house was ripped down.

Finally, we managed to find land we could afford from a friend of my father's, after renting on two other farms first. The land we acquired was essentially bush - African bush (minus the lions of course) with tall grass up to our ears. No electricity or running water and surrounded by tall blue gum trees, that sounded like the ocean when the wind blew them. It required all five of us (my mom, dad, two brothers and myself) to throw some mattresses into the back of my father's old army truck and that's where we slept. My father tied a canvas cover over the top in case it rained. But at no point did I feel sorry for us. This was fun for me. We had been brought up this way our whole lives, essentially trained to be resilient and adaptable. We lived like this, with no electricity or running water for almost a year, with three teenagers and no internet. For the most part we enjoyed it, not once did we complain. We did read a lot of books though!

We helped build our house and plant hundreds of macadamia trees, watering them with a bucket that we filled from a tank at the back of my dad's bakkie (a pickup truck). We learnt by doing, although my only complaint about living in an "Out of Africa movie" was the toilet. I needed one. I can handle everything that life throws at me as long as my ablutions are covered. I was encouraged to shower. My dad drilled holes under a 20-litre bucket, filled it with water and one person would stand on the higher part of our foundation and hold a full bucket of water above the person showering... out in the open... It was breezy! I refused and showered at my friends' houses. Bless my dad, he built the bathroom first! My mother is very intelligent and her problem-solving skills are amazing. She made a kitchen sink out of the frame of a school desk and took a wash basin and slipped it in. In an instant we had a kitchen sink to wash our dishes.

Now, as an adult, I sometimes look into the future and wonder what the hell I'm doing it all for. I keep running in circles to survive - everything gets done at a sprint nowadays - and I get so tired. Then I look back and see how far we've come and realize, we're doing it, we are living. Life is hard but we are in the throes of it now and we seem to be succeeding. We are alive.

My farm isn't a picturesque, well paved, trimmed or treed affair. It's messy, unfinished and our paving is uneven because we laid it down with our own hands. The bushes and weeds always seem to be running the place and there is always a list of unfinished tasks as long as my arm. My clothes are bought from second-hand charity shops (where I know my money is going to a good cause) and I spend my days either barefoot or in gumboots. My husband aspires to a better life, he looks to the future for the both of us. Between us, he is the dreamer and I have my feet firmly on the ground. But I told him jokingly that when his big fancy business trips are finished, he can come "slum" it with me.

There's beauty in living an ordinary life. Not everyone wants the spectacular.

Bee Troubles

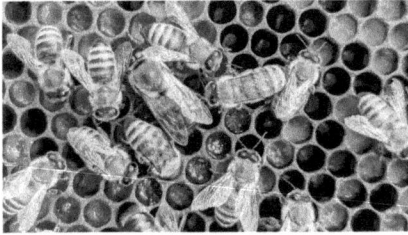

Living on a farm is very different from living in town. Life is busy. I don't recall ever really being bored and now I don't even have time to take up a hobby, write or exercise for that matter. My husband and I have three kids under the age of seven, our eldest has started primary school (which, for a parent new to primary school, is a culture shock of its own). We wake up at four in the morning, to pack lunches, make coffees, get dressed and eat breakfast. It's a half an hour drive to get the kids to school. We live outside of a small town called White River that is another further half an hour's drive from a main city called Nelspruit.

Over the years of growing up on farms, my dad tried many farming enterprises, meaning that as kids we received an amazing, outdoor and hands-on education. He tried growing vegetables in greenhouses. I have a picture of my father holding a cabbage in front of his face - it was as big as his head. He tried farming with cows so we could sell milk, too. I remember a baby calf that used to suck my thumb (I think I was six or seven), I even saw them drain a dead cow they had killed for meat. As a child I took this situation very well and danced around the cow singing "meaty, meat, meaty, meat!" Now however, I would have adopted the cow and never let it be killed. When farming with dairy cows, you wake up at 4am every morning, even on weekends. My dad soon grew weary of this.

A favourite memory of mine and my cousins was strawberry

picking. My father had a huge garden of strawberries surrounded by a fence that kept the dogs out. One day my cousin and I climbed the ladder that went over the fence, determined to eat some strawberries, we came back with our shirts full of strawberries and our shirts pink with juice, grinning with success.

Kids on farms grow up in nature, with an unbridled joy and freedom. I've had the opportunity that few children get, I've handled a baby cow, ridden horses, played with a baby sheep, had a piglet as a pet and even had a gosling follow me around wherever I went because I was its mom and it imprinted on me. Nowadays my community is bees though. Besides our three apiaries, we have one that somehow got into my brother's empty wine barrel. We are still trying to figure out how to extract them with the least number of casualties.

We farm with macadamia nuts, and when it comes to fruit or nut trees (or most farming, for that matter,) it's best to farm in conjunction with bees. We farm with Africanized Honey Bees or better known as the Killer Bee. I've seen videos of bee farmers extracting honey with no suit on at all! That's a honey bee, they can be very placid. Africanized Honey Bees are not so placid, they are extremely volatile and can chase you for kilometers before giving up. Europeans crossbred their Honey Bee with the East African Lowland Honey Bee in order to breed a bee that is more protective of their hive against predators. They just didn't realize how protective. If you get stung too many times you will die. They swarm even if you just stand too close and they don't know you. Yes, bees recognize people.

Our bees drink from a fountain at our front door (the fountain doesn't work and we fill it up every day). They drink a lot of water. My mom and I can fill the fountain with a bucket in the middle of a swarm of bees and they don't sting us. That is one of my favourite things to do. Not many people know what it's like to stand in the middle of a swarm of bees that are just settling back down to drink water. The sound is beautiful ... not so much when they are chasing you and you're running away down a mountain.

Our hives essentially went into a kind of stalled state after my father got sick and passed away. Everything on the farm did. When we finally woke up to the world around us, the hives needed a lot of care. But changing the 'super' to a new one because their hive is falling apart, is a different endeavour. (The main brood box is where the queen bee lives. A queen excluder is a plastic or steel mesh sheet that stops the queen from laying eggs in the top supers. A 'super' is the smaller boxes we add on top of the main brood box where we eventually collect honey from.) The bees don't know us anymore and our bee suites are not up to standard, meaning they are old and full of mold. But besides this, I naively decided to carry on with the plan to update the hive, choosing a triple decker hive straight away. Needless to say, the bees swarmed us, they pressed their cute little bodies against us and stung us right through our suits. My husband ran first (he is terrified of bees and helps me only because he loves me, plus he had three holes in his mesh hat). I ran soon after, racing through the macadamia trees (the branches are great for swatting off bees without killing them). At this point though, I just wanted to drop and roll on the ground.

Once I came to a stop, which wasn't for very long because the bees were still hunting me down, I had to give myself a pep talk on going back to the hive. My bee hive had no lid on anymore and they would get wet if it rained. I ran back, hugged the old super, lifted it off (as bees had now gotten into my mesh hat and were stinging me up my neck), and then got the new super and lid and placed it on top. All this was done a quickly and calmly as I could manage considering they were covering my suit now. I made a run for it again. Bees are so ungrateful sometimes.

When not running from bees, we grow, pick, shell and roast

our own macadamia nuts as well. All this, and the beekeeping is done alone, because we cannot afford to hire help at this stage in the farming business. It is an exhausting, but fulfilling life.

The Best Neighbourhood in the Rainbow Nation

In my opinion I've had an amazing childhood: I've seen and experienced more than most, less than some. I've met people that only see the bad in their childhood, who carry that pain throughout their lives. I have painful memories of awful things that have happened. But after everything I try to remember the good in life. I know my parents were only human and made very human mistakes. My father passed away last year, a man that did everything for his children and never wanted us to leave home or struggle, but he also made mistakes. We are still learning to live without him, without someone to ask for help or reassurance that we are doing the right thing, but we are learning as we go.

To say that my neighbourhood is different from anyone else is not true, everyone has a very unique view of their own neighbourhood. I remain very biased about mine. Because it's the best.

My neighbourhood is a large farming community that drapes down the side of a mountain into a valley made up of many farms. We even have a phone group that we are all part of, and some farmers have formed a neighbourhood watch. We call on them if we get robbed (which has happened to us five times already), as it includes the security company. We brought the police out the second time we were robbed because our caretaker had seen people steal from us and had followed them to their home. The police system is very complicated in South Africa, however. The police arrived to open a case, listened to us and wrote everything down. We explained what our caretaker had seen and said that he could show them where the thieves went. But according to the police this is "hearsay". Two days later the investigator arrived to take fingerprints and photos of broken glass. Again we told him about the caretaker's story and was told he would look into it. Two weeks later I got a message that the case had been closed...but no one had been brought to justice. They broke in another three times after that.

I look at the Government and the general racism in society, and I believe that my generation had a different experience growing up. We were the children of the rainbow nation, when all skin types were (finally) put into the same school class. We grew up together and while I see the colour of people's skin, I find everyone beautiful and my friends are diverse. My child's preschool decided on 'brown or peach' instead of black or white, to avoid the loaded descriptions.

When I was a child, I had a crush on a black boy. I told my father and he said he would disown me. I married a white man by all accounts (I just never told my father he had some Khosa in his lineage.) But my father was a product of his upbringing. We grew up knowing very little of government issues. There was an incident when Nelson Mandela came into power: most white people (sorry, "peach" people) thought he would start a war. My father's reaction was to go out and buy buckets of peanut butter. He wanted to stock up on food for this coming war; I'm sure he stocked up on other foods but the Yum Yum peanut butter tins stand out. In the end, nothing happened of course. We had those cans of peanut better for years, we made cookies and shared bottles with family. I always thought this was hilarious.

I have considered living somewhere else in the world. With my friends telling me their bad experiences or warnings over our failed government. I've tried to look for places that match our weather (not that I hate snow, but I wouldn't want it permanently.) But no place is really home. We have thunderstorms that rattle windows with earsplitting cracks of lightening and sunsets so beautiful you want to paint them (or at least stop the car to photograph them). Where else would I find such friendly people, a nation that just wants to have a beer with a celebrity and not chase them round the block? I'm speaking generally of course. But no one can understand the friendliness until you visit South Africa. Where someone will help push your car if it breaks down or give you a lift to the nearest petrol station without expecting anything in return. Here is home, in the lowveld with my bees and my macadamias and my family and neighbours, and I wouldn't change a thing.

Bristol, UK

4

Escape Goat

BY HANNAH RUMBLE

There is nothing quite as grounding as the scent of another animal on your skin.
SHARON BLACKIE – THE ENCHANTED LIFE

New Year's Day developed into a surreal farce. My husband and I were engaging in the great British tradition of walking off a hangover in the January gloom, joining all the other city-dwelling families in the parks of the city to make this annual *constitutional*. Given we thought we weren't going to be out for longer than an hour, I hadn't given much thought to the appropriateness of my clothing. I was wearing pink tights and a colourful sequined skirt that I had worn the night before to see in the New Year at a neighbour's house party. I just threw on a fleece for good measure as I stepped out the house.

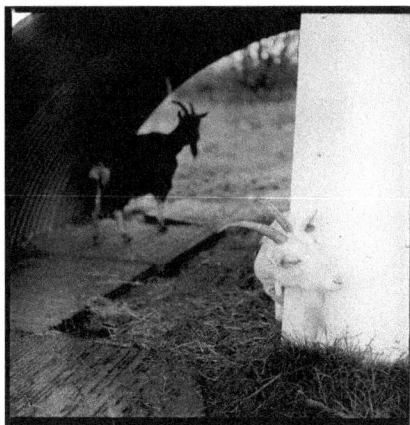

Photo Credit: Eva Frankel

But five hours later we still hadn't returned home. Instead, we were cajoling fourteen goats away from the motorway that bisects the city in two. Our grazing goat herd had escaped from their field beside the motorway by eating through a thicket hedge and jumping over a barbed wire fence. If there's one thing I've learned since becoming a member of an urban micro-diary, goat farming cooperative, it's that goats are very, very intelligent, and very stubborn. They like to demonstrate they have the upper hand to us human herders all the time and they love nothing better than fresh ivy.

The aim of the goat farming cooperative is to connect communities to sustainable food production and regenerative land management. Given it is January in the Southwest of England, there isn't a lot of forage available at this time of year, apart from seasonal evergreens such as ivy. So just as we'd been tempted to overindulge the night before with the New Year festivities, I think the goats had decided they wanted a taste of the seasonal offerings too, being tempted away to overindulge in the freely available and abundant ivy beside the motorway. Subsequently, our New Year's Day walk was turning into a Goat Rescue, and we were utterly unprepared for it.

We had become alerted to the fact that over half our grazing herd were not in their usual field when we decided to just go and check on them as we were passing Bridge Farm – a community site where we kept our herd and milked two goats in the ramshackle old diary that is almost collapsing into the hard shoulder of the motorway. I love Bridge Farm. Until a few years ago, it was just a derelict old farm house with some neglected out buildings nestled under the highway flyover. Then a community collective bought the site with a vision to turn it into a community co-housing site. Since the pandemic, various voluntary groups have been using Bridge Farm for keeping chickens, goats, pigs, growing cut flowers, vegetables and trees from seed. Aside from the various growers groups and animal groups, there's also a purpose built barn for community events and seasonal festivities. Given I live in inner-city Bristol, Bridge Farm is a place that always makes me nostalgic for my rural hill-farming roots. It felt timeless, whilst the madness of the city and constant stream of traffic on the motorway beside it keeps buzzing night and day. It would be quite easy to be a member of the city and never realise what magic unfolds up the driveway to the farm if you didn't stray up it from the busy, noisy, polluted crossroads under the motorway flyover. But if you do, you are rewarded with the magical fruits of various land workers' endeavours.

But back to New Year's Day! My husband and I had to locate some hedge clippers so we could cut through the bramble thicket and locate where the goats had jumped the fence. We needed to follow in pursuit so that we could round them up and bring them back the same way. This involved a lot of rips and holes to skin and clothes from thorns, and a comedy attempt to lure the goats back with us by my husband waving ivy up ahead of them and me chasing the stubborn ones lagging behind with a rake! I felt like we were the main characters in a *Carry on* film. It was well into dusk by the time we got all the goats back into their grazing field, by which time we'd been joined by two other Street Goat members who helped us erect some temporary fencing for the night. I kept giggling at the absurdity of it all and what we must have looked like to the drivers on the motorway at the other end of the field.

I'd stumbled on Street Goat a few years ago when I saw a laminated poster for Street Goat volunteers tied to the allotment fencing near my house. The name grabbed my curiosity so once I reached home, I Googled it and since then, there's been no looking back. My husband and I are now urban goat herders and share the responsibilities of a herd of 49 goats grazing on derelict agricultural or municipal park land throughout Bristol city. The City Council let us graze the goats for free on their land (meaning free forage for the goats), whilst the council get sustainable grazing of their land, so saving money on maintaining the land themselves. It's a delightful win: win.

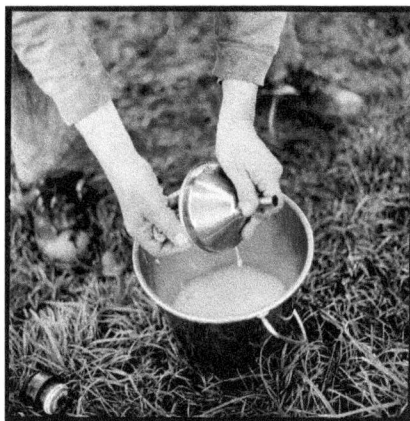

Photo credit: Eva Frankel

Since January 2022 we have been going to Bridge Farm to do a weekly evening milking duty and I also commit to one morning a week feeding them and cleaning out their shelters. At first, we were terribly slow, tentative milkers, but in time, we got faster and be able to use both hands. What delights me, aside from the sweet smell of hay and the intelligence of the goats, is that I have found myself leading two goats to a dairy right beside the M32 highway and its constant hum, in order to get down a pail and sit beside the flanks of Lillian and Betty and milk them. It's such a bizarre contrast! But I am giddy every single time I leave the dairy shed with my litre bottles full of warm, raw, goat's milk. The alchemy of turning it into goat's cheese pleases me immensely. All you need is a litre of warmed-up milk, a squeeze of lemon, a dash of vinegar, a pinch of salt to taste and a then strain the curdled mixture through a muslin over a bowl to catch the dripping whey. After a few hours your soft cheese is ready to eat. I still can't believe I can make cheese so quickly, cheaply and easily and within a couple of hours of returning from milking.

It is a process of care, patience, and nurturing. A beautiful place to arrive at having followed the trajectory of the pandemic, that has landed with a bleat from an animal in my care as I gingerly learn how to milk her. The journey is always the arrival, and as the soil warms up, I am hopeful for the new seeds being planted and the young kids being born to our grazing herd.

To find out more about **Street Goat**, *an urban goat farming cooperative, whose aim is to connect communities to sustainable food production and regenerative land management visit* https://www.streetgoat.co.uk/

Northern Saskatchewan, Canada

5

Girl with the Mistatim

BY MACKENZIE BROOKS

A small girl sits on a brown horse in a red jacket. An older man sits alongside her, a Hudson's Bay blanket under his saddle. They stare out over a lake. The sky is pink, orange, green and yellow. Trees and weeds and globs of paint dot the lake's border; they fade from earthy, muddy, liquid sharpness to lithe gold and russet, magenta and ochre. The scene is wild and tender.

Mistatim is the Cree word meaning 'horse'
Photo: David Krughoff

The scene is imaginary. Horses that far north would be ravaged by blackflies. (There's a reason Weyakwin is called "the swearing place".) And we are north of north. What happened to that painting? I don't know either. I can't remember because I was six. You can't remember because you were a drunk. I know the tenderness is directed from the man to the girl. I know it's us in the painting. I know you put the horses in the painting for me. I couldn't really ride. Neither could you; I was six and you were a drunk – the only way you could ride was if you were tied on. At least that's what everyone says. And it's hard to ride a horse with polio legs.

"He wasn't a mean drunk," they'd say. "You always knew you were loved."

If you hadn't drunk, I'd have understood you, perhaps. You lay down the bottle, and I'll agree to tell you what happens when I'm far-away-in-the-eyes. We could share our art, and you can tell me with that photographic memory of yours what you remember about the scenes that I've only been told of.

We would be friends; I know we are the same. You'd be proud of me. I have produced so many words of art. We would know all these things, if you'd only slowed down for Christ's sake! You were 56. I was 6. I'll never know why you chose the North – I suspect the love of art and the promise of your own radio show. (Also, you couldn't keep a job.) CBC did more than hold a nation together. It held a family together, too.

Those days starting out with the glass of sherry and a few words of Mowat, - merged with cocktails and reams of Shakespeare, and ending with Cosmos and highballs and Gin Fizz and Fitzgerald - produced for you a life of art. Where did that painting go? Where did that life go?

If you hadn't drunk, you would know me; perhaps you'd hardly know yourself. You'd know about the art of my life if you had set aside some time for sobriety. If you'd set aside some time for sobriety, you'd know about my words and my temptation to follow in to that life; my own edge-of-the-sane-world stories.

If you had, we'd know where that painting is.

Regina, Saskatchewan

6

Death is Everywhere, but Sometimes it is Funny

BY ANNABEL TOWNSEND

Part of the "joys" of being determinedly car-less in Saskatchewan is these daily near-death experiences cycling in downtown Regina. (Today's was merely being startled by some oxygen-thief screaming "Get off the fucking road!!" at me while trying to squeeze me into the curb.) Being on two wheels without the motorized metal box around me makes me an interloper invading someone else's space. Vulnerable, outcast, invisible... but it also helps me feel alive, in a strange and messed up way. It gives me ample opportunity to take in my surroundings as well.

Not the worst religious billboard this week.

At the busy intersection of 12th and Albert, the local god-botherers have bought themselves a billboard, on full view to this city's morning commuters. Every few weeks, we get a new religious affirmation to contemplate as we sit at the string of poorly coordinated red lights.

This week's reads

"Anxious?
Rest with Jesus."

I can't imagine I'm alone in interpreting that as a giant advertisement for suicide. What manner of dystopian hellscape is this?

I swerve around a dead squirrel on the road, identifiable as a squirrel only by it's tail. A raven is eyeing it, hungrily. One day, that will probably be me.

The news recently has made me swear off the internet, again. But the doom and gloom is so pervasive, it feels impossible to escape. Gaza, Ukraine, Afghanistan... Covid, the shitshow to the south of us, climate change, wildfires in the Arctic, recession, the dual crises of homelessness and opioid deaths, and even closer to home, trying to parent a trans teen in Scott Moe's Saskatchewan. You cannot detach from any of this and still engage with the world around you.

As I pedal closer to work, an ambulance races past me, sirens blaring. I follow it slowly and I'm greeted by EMS vehicles at the end of our block. No sign of a car crash and no fire truck, so it was probably an overdose. Another one.

Work is frighteningly quiet at first. Dead, even. Stupidly, I check my phone and find that someone I care about is having a mental health crisis and, simply put, doesn't want to be here any longer.

It is all too much today. I find myself getting tearful in the kitchen. I can usually alleviate my misery with sufficient quantities of caffeine and company, but although I have the caffeine, but I could really use a friendly face. Unfortunately, the business hasn't yet developed to the point of having 'regulars'.

But that reminds me — I need to go check the bathrooms and make sure we managed to remove the graffiti. Yesterday someone scrawled something about so-and-so having a huge cock above the toilet in red Sharpie. My pragmatic staff member knew that Sharpie can be removed with hand sanitizer, but I wanted to make sure we got all of it. I cannot for the life of me figure out who scribbled it. Yesterday there were so few folks in, that I should be able to guess who it was. There was one younger girl with a laptop and latte, but I'm fairly sure she never used the bathroom. Then a group of my writer friends came in, all older women who drink tea and write children's books. Finally, there was a little old lady in on her own. She is now my number one suspect, and the mere thought of her writing on the toilet wall makes me smirk uncontrollably. Maybe, at a certain age, you can stop caring about social niceties and politeness. Maybe she just really wanted us to know about the huge cock.

Speaking of the elderly, a trio of older women visit for lunch, and I try my best not to listen in on their conversation in the quiet cafe. I am not successful. One of them is telling her friends about her toy boy, who is fifty years younger than her. I am gobsmacked. And quite impressed. Sugar Grannies are a thing now? Apparently he disappeared for seven months. She assumed he was in jail.

And then I realise they are a book group. This is fictional, and the Sugar-granny is the only one who has read their book. I snort-laugh into my coffee and they glance at me warily.

At last, as if summoned by my subconscious pleas, my friend arrives, and she's even bringing cookies! Girl Guide cookies in fact, as the entirety of her free time is taken up with organising what must be the most progressive Guide troupe in the province. A good friend with good snacks for a good cause. Brilliant.

I tell her about the religious bill board. Are they the 7th Day Adventists? she wonders. Apparently, that group made another ill-advised billboard a few years back, that read

"The best gift a Mother can give is time spent on her knees."

and now I am dying *from laughter.*

I firmly believe that the solution to despair is not hope alone. It is absurdity. There are still beautiful things in the world, amazing, fascinating people, and positive potential futures. They are just more subtle and less sensationalized than all the bad news. When hope and positivity aren't immediately obvious, I look for the absurdity. The world is so, so messed up that sometimes, you just have to laugh at it.

KwaZulu-Natal, South Africa

7

What's the tea, South Africa?

BY LILLY DAUBERMANN

"The grass isn't greener on the other side – "
– RAYMOND B. EAGAN AND RICHARD A. WHIT-
ING,
A PHRASE FROM A SONG THEY WROTE IN 1924.

"The grass is greener where you water it."
– WOLFGANG PUCK.

It's what we make of it.

South Africa is not all that it's cracked up to be. It's not all sunshine and roses. It's full of never-ending corruption, skyrocketing living expenses, high fuel costs, crimes of many magnitudes, and much more. Many citizens complain that with the rising cost of living, their salaries just don't match these price hikes, stressing out many low-, and middle-class households. Not to mention this horrible thing called "Load-shedding". What is load-shedding you ask? Well, for anyone unfamiliar with the term, it is when Eskom (our electricity provider) turns off our electricity anywhere between two and six hours at a time, in different stages throughout the day and night, when there simply isn't enough power to supply each area. Load-shedding started in October 2007 when Thabo Mbeki was in his second term as president. It has not stopped since. Seventeen years and counting. Sometimes the power only goes off once a day, but when the electricity supply is low, we get cut off not just once, but two to four times per day. So, if it's off for four hours at a time, and it goes off four times a day, that equals 16 hours per day! How on earth are we supposed to function with so many hours without electricity?

Many complain that they switch the power off at the most inconvenient times too. 5 am to 7 am is a terrible time. We wake up to darkness. We use some candles, or if you are privileged, you will have some rechargeable lights scattered around your home. Or solar lights that recharge in the sun. You use these so you can see what you are doing, and not fall over everything to go wake up your children, to get everyone dressed, fed, and ready for school and work. The other inconvenient time is 5 pm to 7 pm or 7 pm to 9 pm, when everyone is rushing home after work. The time when parents want to cook a hot meal for their families. It is awful when you are unable to cook because all you have is an electric stove, and gas stoves are beyond your means. If there is money left after paying all the bills, then it usually goes towards buying some take-out. Easy meals on the go. Often, we just resort to some bread with a favorite spread or cold meats.

Those who can afford it have installed solar power systems with inverters for their homes and businesses. But for someone like me solar is unaffordable, so I got myself a small inverter that runs off two deep-cycle batteries and charges when the electricity is on. It can run my Wi-Fi, laptop, fan, and TV when the power goes off, if only for about two or three hours before it runs flat. When load-shedding hits in our area, it affects the towers that supply our Wi-Fi and cellphone signals. They become so unstable that the signal goes off, and then no phone calls can be received or sent out. No internet equals no communication with anyone. It is truly frustrating, and quite dangerous.

Eskom Hld SOC Ltd
@Eskom_SA

#LoadsheddingUpdate

Thursday, 21 March 2024: In order to replenish the low dam levels at the pumped storage power stations, Stage 3 loadshedding will resume from 20:00 tonight until 05:00 on Friday. Thereafter, loadshedding will be suspended again from 05:00 on Friday until 16:00. Eskom will provide an update on Friday afternoon or if any significant changes occur. Unplanned outages remain stable at 14 366MW and planned maintenance slightly increased to 6 307MW. The anticipated electricity demand for this evening peak is 25 672MW.

- Image taken from X/Twitter Eskom, 21 March 2024.

There are apps available like 'Eskom Push' and Load-shedding notifiers that give daily updates like the image above.

As difficult as load-shedding may seem, we have learned to make the most of it. I, for one, have learned not to dwell on the hardships this brings to our country. Instead, the blackouts can become meaningful time spent with loved ones. Times where we play some UNO or board games. We spend more time acquiring the skill to communicate with one another instead of becoming a hostage to our very addictive internet-fueled cell phones. There are far worse problems in our country.

I could sit here and write on and on about all the terrible parts of South Africa, my home country. I have dreamed of leaving this country for the longest time. I want to go see the world and spend time with my family in Canada. (I have it in my heart to immigrate and move there one day.) Or I could visit family in the UK that I haven't seen since I was a baby. Circumstances and finances haven't allowed that for me just yet. So, instead of pondering and swamping my mind with all the negatives of this country, I've adopted the notion that the grass *isn't* greener on the other side. It's *greener where you water it*. I quite like this saying because I believe in looking at things more positively. If you feed your mind, and the company you keep in more positive vibes, your life won't be as miserable as the state of this country. It is what we make of it. I'm a firm believer that what we feed our minds with, is the reality we will live and become.

I've gone through some terrible times in my life; things that no woman should have had to endure. I could have chosen to fill my mind with hate, resentment, and every single negative thought imaginable. I could have kept myself in the slumps. But I decided not to stay there. I cannot just run from all the problems, instead I must find a way to make the most of what I have and become better than I was yesterday. Life is short, so I prefer to live a life well spent and make the most of the time I'm given; where I currently am, rather than wallow in negativity.

The sunnier side of the village

Just outside the town of Newcastle, Kwazulu-Natal South Africa, is a small community we call the Village, Ingagane. It's about a

15km drive from the town of Newcastle. Ingagane has what was once the old Eskom power station. It used to provide electricity to surrounding towns and most parts of Natal. Now it's just an old eerie-looking power station. A rusting reminder of history; a standing monument crumbling away. My children and I are fascinated by the four cooling towers that were once filled with clouds of smoke, fueling the village and surrounding towns with electricity. I often wondered why they closed this power station down. The village was once filled with employees of Eskom, who raised their families there. There used to be a functioning school, public library, swimming pool, bowling club, cricket and rugby clubs, children's parks, and much more. Now, the village has just withered away like the cooling towers of the power station. I wondered why these parts of the village were left to be vandalized and destroyed. It could have still been used by the villagers.

My parents purchased their first house here in Ingagane a few years back, right across from one of the parks where my children often go to play. It is peaceful most of the time and provides me with some tranquility and peace for my soul, away from the hustle and bustle of city life. I am glad that the village didn't become an abandoned ghost town, and that the public were allowed to purchase some of these homes after the mothballing of the power station. I often pondered that if they hadn't decommissioned this power station, maybe we wouldn't have such an electricity crisis like we have had for the past seventeen years.

The village reminds me that people can live in peace and be helpful to one another. The villagers are friendly most of the time. This gives me hope that there is a sunnier side to all the problems this country faces. Regardless of ethnic group, those around here have an amiable, humble approach to life. A kind of help-thy-neighbour philosophy, unique in many ways. Something that fascinates my children about the village is the herd of cows and a few horses that wander the streets and playgrounds of Ingagane, without a care in the world. They are just there grazing. For those animal lovers out there, it's truly a sight to behold. Nobody bothers them, and the cows don't bother the people in the village. They just be there, doing their thing. This is part of what makes South Africa truly unique. To tourists, this is fascinatingly strange, but to us here in South Africa, it's considered normal.

My daughter Abigail standing metres away from the once coal-fuelled power station. Shows us just how magnificent these towers at the old power station truly are.

What's the tea?

There's a local bar in Ingagane that my boyfriend and I often like to go to. I cannot say that it's cozy, but it's rustic and very basic, in the sense that it has some gambling slot machines at the back and two pool tables. It's not pretty, but it's an escape from the stresses of work and life for a short while, and a place to meet up with some friends. We would often play a few games of pool, and once I even got dragged into playing in a competition. We were only three ladies out of ten men who entered, that's why my one friend had begged and squirmed her way into convincing me to play with them. Needless to say, it was fun, even though we ladies lost against the men. The bar is a place to go to get some good (cheapish) ice-cold beers on those extremely hot days, or like me, Jamaican rum and coke.

No town - especially no *small* town - is free from gossip. Nothing is more gossip-worthy than stepping into the local bar. Want to know the local tea? The latest buzz on certain people's lives? Well, then just pop into the local bars here in Newcastle. You will get all the local juicy news, whether you asked to hear it or not. I wouldn't be surprised if I've been the highlight of someone's gossip blitz there. I could be seen holding my father's arm walking into a shopping centre, and then the gossip would go around that I'm dating an older man, and that I'm probably just after his money. Oh, and how people love to add their version of what was told to them! It's rather fascinating that by the time the gossip has done the local rounds, you will be left with a version completely different to the original story.

I have learned not to lend my ears out, nor to believe everything that is said to me. Sometimes all I can do is shake my head, especially if I know the true story. I can just smile or if it truly upsets me, I boil with rage inside listening to others spreading the gossip. Other times I just can't help it and then I run my mouth off defending the person they are gossiping about. I am a peacekeeper; I don't like conflict. But when the time calls for it I like to set things straight. It shuts them up for a while.

But it's not just gossip you hear at the local bars. Lee, our lovely bar lady has become such a great friend over the years. I could also say to some extent she is the bar psychologist. Broke up with your boyfriend? Did you lose your job? Don't want to be left alone? You head down to the local bar, order your drink of choice, and speak your broken heart out. The drink is not the solution, but it can at least make you feel like you are not alone.

That place was my go-to when I just got to Newcastle. I didn't know anyone. And it was close to where I lived at the time. There were no decent coffee shops I could go to in this town where I could sit and meet people. Lee was one of the first people I had met here. She has the friendliest smile and such a welcoming, humble way about her. Always friendly, serves you with a smile, and always asks you how you are doing. Lee just listens, truly sympathizes with you, comforts you, and will encourage you in some way. She's always making sure to tell you that tomorrow will be better than today. Most times she will give you good advice, too. She has a wry sense of humor as well, that helps on those days you feel a little low. The best part about her is she never betrays your confidence, never shares your heartfelt banter with the other customers. She truly is a gem of a bar psychologist. This is how I started meeting new people and getting acquainted with the town. Some very well-to-do people, and some not-so-nice types. I guess we are not everyone's favorite cup of tea, but that's okay.

The gossip that runs around is not exclusive to the local bars. It can be at the workplace, or shopping centres where you run into someone, and they just can't help themselves to just give you the latest juice about something they heard or saw. Some people cannot help themselves. It's how you take it, and what you do with that information that was given to you without you asking.

To my mind, no town or country is perfect. No place is free from atrocities or gossip. Yet every country and town has amazing qualities to it too. Is it going to help thinking that the grass is greener on the other side of the world? Is it better to pick up and leave the country you are in? I used to think it was the better option. But I am learning to stop being negative about our country. It has so much goodness too. I choose to be a positive ray of sunshine, instead of a negative worry wart. We truly have to make the most of what we have.

Lee the "bar psychologist" and I at her son's 21st birthday party at, Rentsels, the local bar.

I will leave you with this thought. Are you watering the grass where you stand? Have you truly taken the time to decide actively and consciously to be the change you want to see in your community? Or would you rather be a part of the problem? Many believe that the grass is greener on the other side, but many fail to see the beauty and treasures they have right where they were planted. Fertilize that. Begin to see that your circumstances can and will change by just choosing to water the grass where you are. No country is perfect, but it can be a mesmerizing place to be if you just tend to it a little. Change starts with you first. I think again of my friend Lee. Would it hurt you to help someone you only just met, as she does? Bringing a smile to someone's face or lightening their burdens just a little by doing one small act of kindness can be just the change that your neighbourhood needs. So yes, South Africa isn't perfect.

But it's a beautiful kaleidoscope of diverse colors and beauties, and I endeavour to embrace that, load-shedding or no load-shedding!

Kennedy, Saskatchewan

8

Home is Where the Cat Is

BY JAMES PARK

I've never owned my own home. I've been living on my own for nearly forty years, and renting all that time. I've never been what anyone would call wealthy, but I've always been able, through diligent budgeting and occasionally blind good luck, to keep a roof over my head. That all nearly changed three months ago.

I've always been worried, when living in apartment buildings, that one of the other tenants would be careless or unlucky, and start a fire. I dreaded the thought of being forced to leave my home through no fault of my own. I realize this may not be something most people worry about, but what can I say, anxiety disorders are a hoot! Anyway, you've probably guessed by now what happened, because you're very clever, and I haven't been very subtle. Let's get into the details then, shall we?

One afternoon in January, around tea time, the smoke alarm in the hall outside my apartment began blaring. I wasn't overly concerned, as this wasn't the first time it'd gone off for seemingly no reason. A quick check in the hall confirmed my belief that it was, in fact, nothing. My son on the other hand was not so easily assured. I looked out of our window, and saw a group of people huddled together, all pointing at the roof of the building.

"Ok, let's go." I said, "This looks serious."

After chasing our two cats around the apartment for what felt like ages, we finally managed to gather them up and head outside to join the crowd. It turned out that an apartment on the top floor, the one directly above us, was engulfed in flames. Fire was shooting about twenty feet out the window, and I barely had time to register what I was seeing before the firefighters herded us all into a neighbouring building, and out of harms way. While we stood huddled in the foyer, unsure of anything. The building managers arrived, and did their best to assure us that everything would be OK eventually. Eventually. Not long after they left, my landlord, the man who owns the condo I'm renting, came and told us that he would put us up in a hotel until everything was sorted. We were very grateful, and a bit surprised that there were pet friendly hotels in town.

We bundled into his car, very disoriented, shaken, but essentially unscathed. While we had only our cats, and the clothes on our backs, we felt certain that we'd be back home in no time, and everything would be back to normal. I had no idea how wrong we were.

We enjoyed the first night in the hotel, treated it like a mini vacation. We watched TV, ordered a pizza, had a grand time living like kings.

After the second night, the shine was starting to come off the whole affair; there was no word from the property managers about a return time, and my landlord couldn't afford to pay for our room any longer. It was then that I did something I was hoping never to do, I called my brother. I hate asking for help, and I especially hate asking family. Help from friends comes without judgment; from family, not so much, at least in my case. Suffice to say, my brother was willing to send me the money to extend our hotel stay, and all it cost was my dignity. After two nights in the hotel though, my son decided he'd rather go and stay with his mother, as she had more room, better food etc, and he took his cat Colin with him. That left my cat Vincenzo and I alone to wait out the time until we could return home.

After two weeks, we finally got word from the property managers, in the form of an email telling us that while there was fire damage to the roof of the building, and smoke and water damage to the rest of the building, it would only be another month until we could go home. While this wasn't ideal, I was glad at least that I was able to stay in a nice hotel, my son had a place he could go where he would be safe, and equally importantly, our cats were safe. I knew that we were extremely fortunate, all things considered, we could very easily have wound up on the streets.

Then came another email a few days later. It seemed that while the clean up crews were doing air quality testing, they discovered asbestos in the walls and ceilings of all of the units. All of it would have to be carefully removed by specialists before anyone could re-enter the building. One month became two, and two became three or four. My brother told me, in no uncertain terms, that he would not be able to help me for another four months. I had no idea what to do, and no idea where Vinnie and I could go. As kind as all of my friends were, and are, no one could put us up for three months or more. Panic started to set in.

Then I got a text from a friend I hadn't spoken to very often. He simply said, "We've got a place you can go, but it's out of town."

I was in no position to be picky, so I gave a very hearty "Yes please!"

He was quick to warn me that the house he had to offer was not ideal, it was very isolated, and the town that it was in was very small, and had no services at all. I said, "As long as there are four walls and a roof, heat, running water, and of course wi-fi, I'll gladly take it."

Within three days, Vinnie and I found ourselves the occupants of a three bedroom house in a small, (*extremely* small,) Saskatchewan town, miles from the nearest restaurant, coffee shop, or grocery store. A quick shopping trip bulk buying at Costco in the city before coming out here was all we needed though, and we're all set to bide our time until we can finally return home. Until then, we wait.

As long as I can have Vinnie with me, I'll be OK, no matter how remote, no matter how secluded, no matter how cut off I am, I'll be alright, because home is where the cat is. Besides, it'll only be another four to six months, or eight, or ten, or...

Shropshire, UK

9

The Purple Balls of Hope

BY CLAIRE TERRILL

In deepest rural Shropshire, on the edge of the Welsh border in the UK, we have built a garden full of oddities, curiosities and follies. Tucked between a main road, the A488 and Hope Brook, between the churchyard and the old petrol station, it is about one acre in size, and most of it slopes down from the road to the stream. It is bisected by a footpath, running from the steps down the bank, across to the footbridge over the stream – which is painted purple.

The empty looking garden as it was in 2014. Ten years have brought many changes.

We have very quiet neighbours - in fact, our land borders a graveyard. From the narrow country road, few of our follies can be spotted except for a couple of deliberate hints at what is beneath, for those actively looking. From the footpath, however, a number of oddities can be seen: large metal birds stroll across the lawn; a small tin chapel complete with bell; a model cow sits chewing cud by the churchyard wall. High on the bank above the lawn, a brightly painted summerhouse houses a swing seat; reminiscent of Norwegian dragon architecture with a dragon carved on the ridge of the roof staring out towards Wales. A miniature Victorian viaduct runs along the bank, parallel to the road, complete with a model train. Another dragon is perched on the roof ridge of the bungalow (also painted green), looking down towards the stream. Metal flowers line a path up to the bungalow, past a reed-fringed pond, in which sits a pile of stone frogs, and a monstrous metal fish with glowing eyes. Steps climb the bank at each end of the pond, and a metal model of the Big Ben clock tower supports a prolific yellow clematis. A giant metal cockerel stands on a tree stump, shouting defiance across the lawn.

We moved to Shropshire in 2001. We chose the house because of its position in the deep, heavily wooded Hope Valley, running north to south through the Shropshire hills. There is a stream crossing the garden marking the boundary of our property, and the garden is on the steeply sloping east side of the stream. The house was a fairly nondescript chalet bungalow, but my husband, Alan, noticed the overhanging eaves and thought with a bit of modification, it could be made to resemble a Swiss Cottage, which was one point in its favour. The other was the potential offered by the garden space to build as many follies as he felt like, a particular passion of his. The sloping site suggests opportunities for landscaping and path–building that the flat field at our former home in Kent never did.

Altering the appearance of the house to resemble a Swiss Cottage was not just a fanciful idea. The house was built in the 1970s, at a time when the UK building regulations were at an all time low, and the house was somewhat insubstantial to say the least. It is timber-framed, with brick gables at either end, but the walls between the timbers seemed to be nothing more than concrete slabs, with a small layer of polystyrene insulation stuck to them. In the damp English climate, and especially in the valley, it was cold. So Alan decided to add a layer of external insulation to the outside of the house, sheltered by the over-hanging eaves, and cover it with pine boarding, making it look more like a log cabin. We stained it bright green, just because we like green, and later Alan cut some new bargeboards for the gable ends, with a series of bats hanging from them – an idea we pinched from a public toilet block in Ellesmere, where their bargeboards were carved with swans.

Picturesque and Romantic Swiss cottages usually have balconies, overlooking a gorge with a wild river racing through it. The stream is not quite a roaring torrent, except when it has been raining hard, but our bedroom window looks out over it, and we thought we could put a balcony there. But we never got round to building a proper one, as the main access to the back of the house was directly underneath the window and any balcony supports would block that access. We compromised with a little cast iron Juliette balcony, made in the shape of a spider's web, complete with spider and fly. On the opposite end of the house, under the apex of the eaves, Alan made a pair of half-open doors, housing a large metal chicken, like a cuckoo emerging from a cuckoo clock. It doesn't crow, though.

The latest, most magnificent beast, is a pangolin I got for Alan's birthday this year. Unjustly blamed by some for the Covid-19 virus, pangolins have not had a good press over the last few years, but they have always been one of Alan's favourite creatures. Pangolina, as she is christened, stands upright about five feet high, with her front legs outstretched as if to embrace an anthill. She is made of metal scales and balances on a rather fine tail and her back legs. We have used up most of the flat areas of the garden, so Alan had to make her a stone platform to stand on from two large paving slabs, to which her back legs and tail are firmly bolted. When the weather improves, he will build her an anthill, and has already found some small metal ants to go on it.

When we first moved in, we hadn't fully understood the extent of the garden. Our predecessor had shown us photos of the land-scaping she had had done to create the garden - involving leveling out the back lawn, and making a grassed terrace around the house, as well as the crazy- paved terrace immediately outside the back door. A public footpath cuts across the garden from the road, down a flight of rough steps, across the lawn to a footbridge over the stream, then up the hill through the woods on the other side of the stream to the school and village hall. (In the UK a public footpath is a path that cuts through private property to provide access to others. They are legal rights of way for pedestrians.)

For the first few years, our neighbour across the road was the local child-minder, and walked a group of children through the garden every day up to the school. Not long after we erected an obelisk - (a memorial to my husband's father and grandfather, and to our son) - on the churchyard side of the footpath, one of the children was heard remarking to her friend

"Oh look, that one's escaped from the churchyard."

Sadly, the children have all grown up now, the childminder has moved away and the local school has closed, as there are not enough children in the valley to keep it open.

The only people to use the footpath now are the local dog-walkers and occasional hikers. We've never worried about people walking through our garden. Those that do have always been pleasant and friendly, and many have been very interested in what we are building. The *"Green bungalow with the garden with Things in"* has become quite a local attraction.

Across the lawn, a dry stone wall separates the garden from the neighbouring church graveyard. Next to it is a metal gazebo, filled with glass and metal butterflies. A bank of rhododendrons hide the top end of the wall and hidden within them is a small rustic hut – the dodo-erie, home to Dorothea, a large dodo, guarding her egg inside the nest in the hut. The hut is built from logs of wood, cut down from the tall leylandii trees that lined the edge of the road.

After trimming the immense leylandiis, we decided we needed to use the remaining stumps (about 20 feet tall) for something. But what? Eventually we hit on an idea: large purple metal balls – the Great Balls of Hope.

The Purple Balls of Hope, from below.

Years ago, I bought three large glass bubbles to float on my pond from a garden centre. Idly scrolling through the internet, I found similar ornamental balls in purple/blue iridescent metal, so we bought two. The third one was another find from a garden centre: a strange stone ball with deep slashes through it which appeared to have no function, but which would suit our purposes admirably. We also bought three large resin flowerpots that we painted purple and upended onto the stumps, providing both protection from the rain for the stumps and something to which Alan could firmly attach the purple balls to. After they were first erected, they slowed the traffic on the main road quite effectively, as drivers slowed to stare up at them, obviously wondering what the hell they were. They have become quite a landmark now.

Well below the Balls, at the bottom of the lawn, the stream forms a sharp curve, almost enclosing a section of the opposite bank to form a small island. A metal bridge, styled like a suspension bridge, with goose-head shaped tops to the uprights, spans the stream, giving access to the island. A mountain goat peers at you from the bank, and tucked into a hollow in the bank is a wood- lined temple, the ridge pole of the roof formed by a trunk of a yew tree, growing out of the bank. It is called the Goat Temple, and has small wooden Ionic pillars supporting the triangular pediment. These are shaped like curly goats horns (Ironic) and the pediment is slightly skewed – an Impediment!

Another path leads away from the lawn, following the curve of the stream towards more follies. The stream is half hidden by a canopy of trees, but opposite the end of the house, a small beach has formed. A small concrete rowing boat is moored to the side of the stream, with a marble seahorse perched on the prow, facing upstream.

A giant mosaic tortoise is seated on the bank - and this was by far our most ambitious project. Beneath the tortoise is a doorway, leading into an underground chamber, complete with bats, spiders, and ghoulish heads and large enough to walk through. An arched tunnel curves away into the darkness, at the end of which two steps take you up into the base of a wooden tower, shaped like a Canadian grain elevator.

Climb the stairs inside and at the top you are on a level with the treetops, and a small room feels like being in a treehouse. Perched on the roof of the tower is a large vulture. The doorway opens onto a wooden bridge, leading onto the top lawn, where there is a 450-year old oak tree. Another flight of steps ascends the steep bank to an ornamental arch, giving access to a secret walk behind a high laurel hedge.

Hanging from a lower branch of the oak tree is a Victorian bird cage, but no bird will enter this as it is occupied by a strange creature known as a *bogwoppit*, a mythical creature captured from its normal habitat of drains. It resembles an owl, but has blue webbed

feet and a very mournful expression. (Bogwoppits were first intro-
duced in the seminal work by Ursula Moray Williams in her 1978
book of the same name).

The tortoise/tunnel/tower complex is of course Alan's main folly
in our Shropshire garden, but they were completed several years ago,
and the urge to build hasn't left him. The more recent structures are
on a smaller scale, and whether they count as follies is debatable,
but they are still odd or curious structures, and not the kind of
things most people put into their gardens.

Lucky as we are to have time, space, creativity and amenable - or
at least, very quiet - neighbours, the building continues. This year
will see a shellhouse finished for our pet tortoises, and the anthill
for Pangolina constructed. I have no idea what else Alan may take
into his head to build next, but there will be something, and it will
be slightly odd. Ideas continue to pop up out of nowhere.

The Purple Balls of Hope, as seen from the road.

The garden is private, only accessed by the public footpath, but if you would like to view all of it, look out for The Purple Balls of Hope, and knock at the door of the green bungalow. We will happily show you round.

Regina,
Saskatchewan

10

Imaginary Village, Fictional Small Town

BY PAUL DECHENE

I live in an imaginary village.

It's called the Cathedral Village, a reference to the Roman Catholic, Holy Rosary Cathedral which sits in our community's commercial heart. It's spires figure in logos, posters, tourism ads.

Officially, in our Neighbourhood Plan, written in 1987, we have a practical, bland name: the Cathedral *Area*. But every spring we host a week-long festival celebrating music and creativity that attracts thousands of people and from the first event 30 years ago, it's been known as the Cathedral *Village* Arts Festival.

The Street Fair at the Cathedral Village Arts Festival
Credit: Annabel Townsend

I joined our community association shortly after moving here in 2007. I remember the issue of buying a new domain name for our organization's website came up at one of my first meetings and we settled on cathedralvillage.org with almost no debate. Someone concluded the discussion with, "We *are* a village."

But we aren't. Not really. Cathedral is a community of over 7,000 people sitting just to the west of Regina, Saskatchewan's downtown. To visitors from elsewhere, we're hardly a village but rather one of the city's most urban areas. Cathedral was one of the earliest residential neighbourhoods to be built with successive rings of suburbs growing out from it.

Regina has a population of over 230,000, meaning it isn't at all tiny; it's a perfect example of a mid-sized city. In fact, we dwarf the largest cities in the American states directly to our south: North

Dakota's largest cities are Fargo at 133,000 and Bismark at 75,000; Montana's Billings is a mere 117,000 and Missoula comes in at 73,500. And yet, Saskatchewan is an agricultural province and many Regina residents grew up in small towns, and have family who still farm. As a result, despite the city's size, a country sensibility colours everything here. All our markers of municipal identity are related to those rural roots. We talk about the "Two Degrees of Regina"; that is, how everybody knows or is related to each other or to somebody else you know well. We talk about how we're a great place to raise kids, how you can drive anywhere in town in under 20 minutes, how our friendly, down-to-earth people are our greatest strength.

The longer you live here the more you become like a second-ary character in a Hallmark Holiday movie explaining yourself to the New York lawyer who's about to learn the true meaning of Christmas.

So quaint.

All that is to say, Cathedral is an imaginary village in a city that pretends to be a small town.

If my tone leads you to think I am making fun, I am not. We all inhabit our own fictions. I present this picture of Cathedral to provide background, because, as Regina has grown, Cathedral's identity as a "village" has been constantly challenged — not least by that most big city of all challenges: car traffic.

You can see this in that 1987 Cathedral Area Neighbourhood Plan which says in the section on traffic and parking:

"The most important issue for Cathedral Area residents is traffic management in the neighbourhood. Specific concerns are pedestrian safety, level of non-local traffic movements, speeding and on-street parking."

Many of the solutions offered in that Plan are mere band-aids: reclassifying some streets, adding some traffic lights. Other were never implemented: adding cul-de-sacs and one ways to pre-vent short cutting, narrowing intersections, adding centre medians. Some were built then removed years later: traffic diverters on a pair of residential through-roads.

By the time I moved here in the late 2000s, Cathedral's grid of streets had few obstacles to impede the flow of traffic. The main commercial artery, 13th Avenue, had timed lights at its east and west gateways, a third halfway along its length where it intersected with another main road. Crosswalks with beg-button-activated lights had been set up at the neighbourhood's grocery store and in front of the eponymous cathedral. There was an additional, uncontrolled crosswalk elsewhere but the signage for that was laughably dilap-idated and the painted markings were so faded that drivers often ignored it.

For a straight, 1.6 kilometer long street through a shopping dis-trict, these traffic controls were minimal — especially considering 13th Avenue's four lanes are quite wide and thus, in the evenings when traffic is low, the street's design urges drivers to step on the gas.

Adding to the perils, 13th Avenue lacked any kind of traffic control at an intersection boasting a popular ice cream shop, mean-ing, all summer long young people would be running back and forth through traffic. Further, on-street parking is allowed on both sides of 13th Avenue for much of its length, thus creating obstacles for sightlines. Nighttime visibility was becoming a problem as a canopy of mature elm trees had overgrown many of the street lights, while the aging streetlights themselves were growing dim in some areas.

Meanwhile, in the late 2000s, Regina city council gave the go-ahead for construction of a massive new suburb named "Harbour Landing" to the southwest of Cathedral Village. This was during a period of rapid population growth for the city and Harbour Land-ing achieved full build-out in record time. By the early 2010s, traffic volumes through Cathedral exploded as it became clear that 13th Avenue had become a main route for traffic travelling between this new suburb and downtown and other employment centres.

To anyone who had to cross Cathedral's streets, it was obvious that the traffic volumes were becoming a safety concern.

And then, in 2023, two pedestrians were killed by drivers in two separate incidents on 13th Avenue. Both fatalities happened at night, when cars were more likely to be travelling at or beyond the speed limit and when the street-lighting issues were a problem. One of those killed was an adult man crossing at one of 13th's beg-button crosswalks. The other incident happened nearby, the victim being a 16 year old boy. Few details of his death were ever released by police but the most reliable stories indicate the boy was crossing late at night near the crosswalk but not in it.

Neither driver was charged with an offence and both fatalities were labelled "accidents."

Regina faces traffic injuries and fatalities at a rate comparable to other Canadian cities. But to have two deaths occur so close to each other in the same year — and in the heart of Cathedral, which prides itself on being a walkable "village" — the sense that something was going wrong was widespread.

On social media and behind the scenes at city hall, the councillor for the area was calling for city staff to install traffic calming measures immediately at the intersection where the fatalities occurred. And the community was united in that something needed to be changed on 13th Ave to protect the lives of pedestrians.

The tragic, stupid, horrible irony here, though, is that in the background, Regina's city administration had been working on a Vision Zero plan for the preceding two years. This was meant to be a design framework that would mitigate the risks of incidents exactly like these.

Officially, Vision Zero is a set of strategies around street and neighbourhood design that strives to reduce the number of road injuries and deaths to zero. It was first devised in Sweden in the 1990s and has spread out from there to cities across Europe and into North America. But more than a strategy, adopting a Vision Zero framework represents an intentional philosophical shift among its city administration where they stop accepting a certain amount of bloodshed as an inevitable result of moving cars about efficiently. In every decision related to transportation, when traffic engineers and city planners are balancing human lives against travel times, human lives become the priority. The goal isn't to minimize deaths, it's to make it so that they never happen.

By every account, wherever a Vision Zero philosophy has been adopted, cities have seen dramatic reductions in road injuries over time. In fact, in 2019, early adopters of Vision Zero, Oslo and Helsinki, reported zero traffic fatalities.

Regina, then, was following a well-established urban planning trend and living up to another it's oft-repeated ruralisms: *We're 20 years behind everywhere else.*

City administration, including the team who were working on Vision Zero, had taken notice of 13th Avenue's death toll. How could they not? These tragedies were felt city wide but, more point-edly, many city staffers live in the Cathedral neighbourhood. These incidents happened in their backyard. As a result, the Vision Zero team decided to include a measure specific to Cathedral in their recommendations to council. On March 27, 2024, they presented this measure to city council at an executive committee meeting: it proposed that the entirety of Cathedral should become Regina's first "Community Safety Zone" in which the speed limit on all roads would be lowered from the city-wide standard for residential zones of 50km/hr down to 30km/hr. They pointed out that as Cathedral is primarily residential neighbourhood with three elementary schools, a grocery store and a commercial corridor through its middle, it has some of the highest year-round pedestrian traffic in the city. A slower speed limit was a natural fit for such a walkable community.

The team also noted that while this Cathedral Community Safety Zone had been devised as part of their two-year long development process for Vision Zero, they had been planning to roll out that specific recommendation a year into the framework's lifecycle — that is, in 2025. But with the 13th Avenue fatalities, they decided it was worthwhile to bring it forward a year earlier and include it in the launch of the framework itself.

Central to their 30km/hr recommendation is the obvious conclusion that when a car collides with a human being, lower vehicle speeds result in fewer fatalities. It is also noted within the scientific literature that if you graph a curve relating car speed to the risk of pedestrian fatality, the line you get is not linear. When a car is travelling at one or two kilometres per hour, pedestrians will survive virtually every time. Then, as speed increases to 60km/h and beyond, the line curves towards 100 percent, where every single collision causes a pedestrian fatality.

And it is right around 30km/hr where that curve representing risk from a collision stops increasing gradually and begins to arc sharply towards death.

The Canadian Association of Road Safety Professionals lists the approximate survival rate of pedestrians hit by a vehicle travelling at 50km/h at two out of ten people while eight will most likely die from the collision. At 40km/h that climbs to six out of ten surviving while four die. At 30km/h, the survival rate shoots up to nine out of ten people while only one will die.

It is for this reason that, by 2023, many cities in Europe had already dropped speed limits in their residential neighbourhoods down to 30km/h. And while Toronto, as of this writing, is also in the process of reducing their residential speed limits to 30km/h, many other Canadian cities — such as Edmonton, Kitchener, Hamilton and Calgary — are only reducing theirs to 40km/h.

The marked increase in survivability at a 30km/h speed limit was definitely listed as the primary motivation behind their more-European recommendation. But, when questioned by council about why city administration was recommending the adoption of a Vision Zero framework for the city, a lead member of the team became visibly emotional when answering:

> "Obviously, whether it's city administration, whether it's the Regina Police Service, we have to handle the requests that come in when people have lost a loved one. And it was challenging to tell people to their face that that was an inevitable outcome of a transportation system that moves vehicles efficiently. And when we look at other jurisdictions, we see that they've been successful in actually bringing [fatalities] down. And so we were looking at what's successful and wanting to replicate that here so we don't have to continue having those conversations with residents."

It was an reminder of how tragic incidents like the fatalities in Cathedral have far reaching consequences.

Once the administration's recommendation to lower speed limits in Cathedral became public, something remarkable happened. The cliché of a village, of a small town, is that the residents there aren't exactly friendly to change. And you would expect that this would hold true in Regina. We're a winter city in the midst of the vast expanse of the Canadian prairie. People here love their vehicles — especially their trucks. You would think that there would be massive negative outcry about any effort to curtail Reginans' vehicular freedoms.

But at first, that didn't happen.

I mean, it did *eventually*. But initially, the conversation was refreshingly well-informed and open to making changes that would save lives.

On social media and at in-person public engagement events, there was widespread and vocal support for the speed limit reductions, with many people saying the change was overdue. Both the local community association and the Regina Police Service supported the change. And the city councillor for the area, Andrew Stevens, quipped during executive committee, "Man, I'll take a thousand angry calls because someone has to go 30 rather than taking calls about someone dying."

It was looking very much like the Vision Zero Framework and the Cathedral Community Safety Zone would be approved by city council when they met in April. But at that March 27 executive committee meeting, Councillor Stevens went on to predict where things were heading:

> "Not infrequently, when we have this conversation, whether it's in school zones or elsewhere, the 'traffic-deaths-are-inevitable' constituency comes out. That's my worry. That's the public opinion that hasn't been heard here. And I don't need to hear it anymore."

Right on schedule, as soon as the Vision Zero recommendations were reported more widely in local media, out came that 'traffic-deaths-are-inevitable' constituency.

The arguments on social media were pretty much what you'd expect: "Pedestrians and cyclists need to take responsibility for their own safety." "People need to get off their phones." "This isn't about safety, it's a cash grab." "Enforce a jay walking bylaw, not punish drivers." "Pedestrians need to respect that streets are for cars." "Maybe we need mandatory 'Look Both Ways' classes for Cathedral hippies."

There were threats to never shop in Cathedral again, to drive through the neighbourhood honking horns, to simply ignore the new speed limit.

And in some corners of Facebook, the discourse even drifted into 15 Minute City conspiracy theories where the posters claimed the speed limit reduction was the first step towards a Big Brother dystopia where people would be restricted to zones and fined for leaving them.

This shift in prevailing public opinion had an impact on council as evidenced by the much softer support for the Cathedral Community Safety Zone at their follow-up meeting on April 24, 2024.

Support for the Vision Zero framework part of the recommendations remained unanimous — no doubt, primarily because it made no specific street-level changes or budget demands in the short term.

The debate on the Cathedral Community Safety Zone, however, could best be described as *byzantine*, involving multiple levels of amendments, councillors doing amateur traffic engineering and hilarious procedural SNAFUs ("Situation Normal: All Fucked Up.") In the end, the Community Safety Zone was narrowly approved in a six to five vote, but only after the speed limit recommendation had been raised from 30km/h to 40km/h.

It was the compromise council could live with.

And while administration's original recommendation would have likely saved more lives over the long term, Vision Zero and the Community Safety Zone offer more than just speed limit changes. As I write this, city crews are installing curb extensions at intersections along 13th Avenue which narrow the distance that pedestrians have to traverse when crossing the street. They are also adding mid-street caution signs to remind drivers about crosswalks. By narrowing the driving lane, they are forcing drivers to drive slower.

Administration also says they are lobbying the provincial crown corporation, SaskPower, which governs street lighting to clear away some of the foliage and improve light brightness.

The 40km/hr signs are coming and enforcement of the new speed limit will begin in two weeks.

Ironically, when you look at the construction, the curb extensions, the extra signage, Cathedral Village is looking more urban now than it did a few weeks ago. And that's okay. The kind of village that Cathedral aspires to is itself a fiction. It's a storybook village. It's Hobbiton or Bree, a close-knit, friendly place where, apart from the occasional Ringwraith intrusion, you can feel safe, raise a family, maybe write a book about your adventures.

By tackling our big-city traffic problems, we're maybe a little closer to that ideal today, despite all the urban trappings and internet arguments over urbanism.

The "village" in Cathedral Village was always a state of mind.

The End

Contributors

Mackenzie Brooks

Mackenzie is a freelance writer and has been writing for clients since 2008. She loves people and storytelling. Her own story has many chapters - some are introspective, some are chapters of adventure and discovery. All are chapters with big personality. Her home is on the prairies, but she is a world citizen with many more chapters to write.

Mackenzie Brooks

Lilly Daubermann

Lilly is a devoted mother of three, nature enthusiast, Health Sciences student and former educator. Her journey unfolds through the chapters of nurturing, teaching, learning, and embracing the beauty of nature, family, and personal growth. In her spare time, Lilly immerses herself in the world of literature and writing. She finds joy and fulfillment in the written word. Through her writing, she shares her experiences, insights, and dreams with the world.

Lilly Daubermann

Paul Dechene has been watching Regina city council for entirely too long and reporting on their meetings live to social media for only slightly longer. He is co-host of the Queen City Improvement Bureau on 91.3FM CJTR, Regina community radio.

Paul Dechene

Erin Derfoldy is a multifaceted individual, thriving as a devoted mother, passionate beekeeper, and driven businesswoman. Residing on the picturesque farms of the Lowveld in South Africa's Mpumalanga region, Erin's life is deeply rooted in the natural world. As an avid learner, she embraces new skills with enthusiasm, from apiculture to culinary arts. Through her writing, Erin shares her wisdom, wit, and warmth, offering a glimpse into her extraordinary life and the lessons she's gleaned along the way.

Erin Derfoldy

Cara Amy Goldthorpe is a writer, mystic, holistic health practitioner, and former lawyer. Her storytelling is inspired by her diverse life experiences. Cara's life took a drastic turn after being locked down in Costa Rica during the Covid-19 pandemic – when she decided to quit law and begin a new path, devoted to her creative passions as well as studies of holistic health (including indigenous medicines of Central America). She is currently working on developing a community centre and healing sanctuary in Southern Costa Rica.

Cara Amy Goldthorpe

James Park

James has been living in Regina for the last 25 years or so, but he's originally from Northwestern Ontario. After years of little to no success at a series of dead end jobs, James has finally decided to make the leap, and take on the life he feels he was meant for, Bohemian Vagabond! The pay isn't great, but the hours are fantastic!

Oh, sometimes he writes too.

James Park

Leighton Peart

Leighton is one of our copy editors at Pete's Press, and also a content writer and SEO Specialist in Toronto. More of his work can be found on medium.com/@LeightonPeart

Leighton Peart

Hannah Rumble

Hannah has some unusual hobbies that she likes to indulge in, outside of her work mentoring 14 -18 year olds with caring responsibilities. She plays in a gamelan orchestra, is a goat herder, and travels - everything from hiking European trails to escaping to sea under the sail of a tall ship as often as possible. You could say she's all about gongs, goats and grueling journeys! She lives in Bristol with her husband and an allotment full of veggies.

Hannah Rumble
photo: Eva Frankel

Claire Terrill

Claire spent the working part of her life teaching small children; later teaching adults and their children together. In the last ten years she's been happily retired and spends her days reading, knitting, sewing, writing and dreaming up new ideas for the house and garden which her husband then carries out. She has written two books about the houses she has lived in and about the follies she and her husband have built. Claire also regularly gives talks on a range of subjects connected to Science and Architecture.

Claire Terrill

*Write the Neighbourhood was curated and edited by
Annabel Townsend*

Annabel Townsend
Photo credit Maple Baxter

Annabel regularly has to explain why she chose to emigrate to Saskatchewan, but it was on the Prairies where most of her ambitions became reality. After graduating with a PhD in coffee, she has opened several coffee-and-book-related small businesses on both sides of the Atlantic. When not dealing with an unpleasant amount of business spreadsheets, she cycles, and writes nonfiction pieces usually about failure and hope. She lives in Regina with her husband, kids and a menagerie of small furry critters including Pete the Cat, who lends his name to this publishing company.

www.ingramcontent.com/pod-product-compliance
Lightning Source LLC
Chambersburg PA
CBHW051248020426
42333CB00025B/3107